Depression
SELF HELP

How to break
through depression

Revised and Updated Edition 2020

Alfred Bellanti

DEPRESSION SELF HELP
"How to Break to Through Depression"
Alfred Bellanti
Revised and Updated Edition November 2020

Paperback ISBN: 978-0-6489582-3-9

Book Interior and E-book Design by Amit Dey

Copyright © Alfred Bellanti 2020

Disclaimer: Every care has been taken to ensure that the knowledge and techniques in this book are workable and safe. Success using this knowledge and techniques may vary from person to person depending on how well the knowledge is applied and how thoroughly the exercises are done. The book is very helpful but is not intended as a total substitute for consultation with a mental health practitioner.

Follow the blogs and articles on www.howtotreatdepression.org

Table of Contents

Introduction

This pandemic has caught many of us unaware and created depression due to unemployment, lockdowns, quarantines, self-isolation and restricted movement or travel. Let me tell you how much I empathize with the way you are feeling right now. You are probably wondering how the hell this book is going to help you beat your depression so I'll tell you why! It's because I've spent many years in that godforsaken state myself, that's why! Therefore continue to read this book because at least one of the scenarios I cover will apply closely to your case.

In this book you will find ways to avoid depression taking you over completely. You will learn more about depression so that you can become more objective about it. You will discover ways to lift you out of your current depression. You will learn about ways that have been proven to increase happiness. You will learn about the types of treatment available and You will learn what you can do to help yourself.

I know that when you are depressed you view the world through a depressed state and nothing seems to hold interest or present any joy for you. I also know that when you are depressed your self-esteem can plummet and you can feel worthless. You can come down on yourself so heavily that you could start to believe no one wants to know you. In turn you withdraw into yourself and isolate yourself. That makes your depression worse by precipitating you into a downward spiral from which there seems no way back.

Retrospective self-analysis taught me that there is a point at which the depressed state takes over. It is a kind of letting go, either consciously or unconsciously. When the letting go occurs you start sinking down into that depressed state. Then in that low state it becomes more and more difficult to see a way out.

It's pretty much like if you were out on a boat in the middle of the ocean and the boat sinks. You find yourself in the water and manage to get hold of a lifebuoy and you start hanging on, and keep hanging on, hour after hour, hoping for rescue. Then you get tired of hanging on, and it becomes harder and harder to hang on, so tired in fact that you can't hang on any longer, and you let go.

You let go either because you're too tired to hang on any longer or because a momentary lapse of awareness causes you to lose your hold. Either way you begin to sink down into the depths and get caught in the depths … and you can drown! Many years ago I "drowned" because I didn't know better. Has this happened to you?

If it has then **don't despair**! Before "drowning" and even from the depths of the ocean you can look up through the water to the sky and you can see the light above. You must believe there will be better days ahead. I know this is difficult when you are in the depths of despair but take my word for it; there will be better days ahead.

During one of my darkest moments, a friend told me "You'll look back at all this one day and laugh". I found it hard to believe him at the time, and shrugged off his suggestion. I didn't believe him. The fact is that years later, when we recalled those days we did laugh!

Even in the darkest tunnel, there is a light at the other end. Let yourself be drawn to the light, rather than get stuck in the darkness.

You and Your Depression

If you are managing to read this book you are likely not as depressed as you think. Let me guess now. At best you are managing to hold down a job and you go through your tasks with a heavy heart just because you have to earn a living, you have to pay the bills.

Possibly you cannot concentrate like you did before therefore performing your tasks becomes more difficult than it used to be but you hang in there, necessity demands it.

If you are unemployed then the situation is different because you are really struggling and have to survive on basics; maybe getting help from family, friends or charities. Even under these conditions you can maintain dignity and self respect.

Another scenario: You are at home and the place is in a mess, the dishes are piling up, there's washing to be done but you find that the motivation is lacking. You possibly find it hard to get out of bed, and when you do, you drag yourself around. You look at last night's dirty dishes still in the sink and look away, but wherever you look there's cleaning or tidying to do. You spend most of the time in your pyjamas or night gown, maybe smoking cigarette after cigarette knowing there's work you have to do but you can't get yourself to do it.

Or maybe you feel a little better than that, and you manage to get yourself to the shower some time during the day, get dressed and do a bit then sit down again. If you live alone, depression can feel worse for you. If you are in a good relationship then when your partner comes home that can provide some relief. But the next day when your partner leaves for work you feel down again.

It's hard to look forward to the following day because you believe you will feel the same again. If you are in a bad relationship, then you can find no relief, even when your partner comes home.

Now we come to that very deep type of depression that stops you dead in your tracks! It immobilizes you completely! You go to sleep at night and wish that you never wake up. You've tried and tried to make a go of your life but nothing seems to work out for you. This can happen for financial reasons or if your wife, husband, girlfriend or boyfriend has left you or if someone close to you has passed away. You will read more about grief in a later chapter.

Whatever scenario you are in, the suggestions, techniques and solutions in this book will apply to you.

I remember a time in my life when I was so depressed I could no longer face going to work. I was so unhappy that I felt annoyed when people around me were happy. "What have they got to laugh about?" I was asking myself. I would look at elderly people struggling in pain on crutches and walking frames and wonder what it was that kept them going when all I wanted to do was die!

Feeling like this you begin to shun people, become withdrawn, reclusive, lose your self esteem and sink deeper into your misery, become more self-absorbed. You are in a state of depression and there is a dark comfort within there, it is safe. You no longer try therefore you can longer fail. You stop getting involved with people then you won't be hurt by them anymore. Why look for a job? Why go to work? You don't even want to be alive. Why trust anyone anyway? You always get hurt.

Many deeply depressed people have trouble getting out of bed in the morning because their day holds nothing for them. In this case, getting out of bed becomes the first challenge! People who are not depressed often can't understand depression at all. They'll say things like: "Snap out of it!", "Get over it!", "Don't worry, you'll be ok." Until you experience long term depression and unless you've suffered from it, it's hard to believe what I'm talking about.

When you are deeply depressed you look around you and see yourself living in a world where you feel you don't belong. You wonder how everyone else gets up and faces the day filled with enthusiasm and the urge to get going while you have to work extra hard to even get out of bed and take a shower!

Every little task seems daunting. You lose concentration. You do what you do because you have to do it, but nothing ever feels right. There is an underlying yucky feeling that never goes away no matter how hard you try to shake it. No matter how many books you read about it. No matter how many doctors you talk to about it and even the pills you've tried over the years do nothing for you anymore.

You begin to feel that this is just how your life will always be. You've stopped talking to friends about your feelings and have decided to accept them and keep them to yourself. It's hopeless! You see no future. Every day is a total misery. You wish you could die because death would bring certain relief.

However chances are that if you are feeling this bad you wouldn't be reading this article. You wouldn't have even switched on your phone, tablet or computer, is that right? But because you are reading this it means that you are well enough and motivated enough to do something about it! You are taking responsibility for your state, and that's what it is! A state! You have been in a happy state before, or a moody state, or a thoughtful state, now you are in a depressed state.

Therefore keep reading, find out more about your state, what could be causing it and more importantly learn proven techniques that will help you overcome it.

Major Depressive Disorder

For this book I have chosen Major Depressive Disorder for my topic. Major Depressive Disorder (MDD) is the most common severe depression. It is sometimes called Clinical Depression. There are many subtypes. The subtypes will be covered under a new title in future.

I do not recommend self-diagnosis and have included the more common symptoms for MDD for educational purposes only.

List of Symptoms:

1. Depressed mood most of the day nearly every day

2. Markedly diminished interest in pleasure in all or almost all activities most of the day, nearly every day

3. Significant weight loss or weight gain when not dieting, or decrease or increase in appetite nearly every day

4. Insomnia or hypersomnia

5. Psychomotor agitation or retardation nearly every day as observed by others

6. Fatigue or loss of energy nearly every day

7. Feelings of worthlessness or excessive or inappropriate guilt nearly every day

8. Diminished ability to think or concentrate, or indecisiveness, nearly every day

9. Recurrent thoughts of death, recurrent suicidal ideation without a specific plan, or a suicide attempt or a specific plan for committing suicide

A qualified clinician must exclude other factors before evaluating the above symptoms. Once those factors have been excluded then at least five of the above symptoms, which include 1 or 2, must have been occurring during the same two week period. The diagnosis of Major Depressive Disorder can then be decided.

Explanation of Above Symptoms:

1. This is fairly straightforward: Feeling depressed most of the day almost every day.

2. The medical term for this is anhedonia; it means loss of pleasure in things previously found pleasurable. This could include eating, sexual activity or other recreational activities.

3. Again, this is fairly straightforward: Marked weight loss or weight gain and increase or decrease in appetite.

4. Lack of sleep, badly disrupted sleep or too much sleep.

5. Agitation is like restlessness, retardation is slowing down.

6. Feeling very tired with no energy.

7. Feeling unworthy of anything, feeling guilty or very guilty whether there is a real reason or not.

8. Unable to concentrate or make decisions.

9. Thinking about death or seriously thinking about suicide.

    1. Major Depressive Disorder Subtypes - There are five defined subtypes of MDD: *Melancholic Depression*

    2. *Atypical Depression*

    3. *Catatonic Depression*

    4. *Postpartum Depression*

    5. *Seasonal Affective Disorder (SAD)*

The most common time of onset for MDD is in a person's twenties and thirties with females affected about twice as often as males. MDD affected approximately One hundred and sixty three million people (2% of the world's population) in 2017. The percentage of people who are affected at one point in their life varies from 7% in Japan to 21% in France. Lifetime rates are higher in the developed world (15%) compared to the developing world (11%).

No need to be discouraged by these statistics. You will soon be out of your depression by continuing to read this book, doing the recommended exercises and applying the techniques.

What About You?

How would you rate your depression on a scale of one to ten? Circle the number as it applies to you Where 1 = No depression and 10 = Suicidal.

1   2   3   4   5   6   7   8   9   10

How did you score? Here is a guide:

    1 = No depression

    2 - 3 = Mild depression

    4 - 6 = Moderate depression

    7 - 9 = Severe depression

    10 = Suicidal.

What was your score? **If you rated yourself at 10**, ge**t yourself professional help immediately**!

If you rated yourself between 7 and 9, professional help is recommended.

If you scored anywhere in between 3 and 6, you should be able to help yourself.

If you rated 1 or 2, you are not depressed, so get off this page and keep reading.

True Cases

1 I remember walking with a friend of mine Gary during one of my states of depression except that he was much more depressed than I was. He had lost his wife only 18 months after their wedding. She committed suicide. I encouraged him to come for a walk because I had to do something to help him. I thought walking and talking may have helped.

We were walking along a road that ran alongside a port in a bay. There were storage depots, cranes, containers and ships. Then there was the water in the bay and beyond the water, the horizon, and a postcard perfect sunset.

The cranes, storage depots, containers and ships silhouetted picturesquely in the foreground added to this scenery. My friend Gary was understandably preoccupied in his depressed state; he didn't see the sunset until I pointed to it.

As I pointed I said to him: "You know Gary, I get depressed too, and then I see something like that and I see the sun shining from the distance through all this man made stuff. It gives me a glimmer, a small, small glimmer of hope, the tiniest spark within; and I grasp that spark and it helps carry me through, because that spark can grow!'

I then asked Gary if there's anything he wanted to talk about it and I would try to help him with it. He replied "No, it's ok; you've cheered me up already!"

The tragedy with depression is that when you are in a depressed state, your outlook is depressed. You can neither perceive or feel, nor experience anything as joyful. Your outlook for the future is gloomy. You can easily convince yourself that you will never feel any other way. In the extreme your outlook can seem so gloomy and hopeless that you can convince yourself that suicide is the only way out. Nothing could be further from the truth. Here is an example:

2. I once worked in a hospital psychiatric ward where one of the patients had been admitted after having been saved from jumping over a cliff. He was lucky! The police had rescued him before he took the leap into eternity. After having been in the ward a couple of days the patient asked me "do you think it's right that a person should be stopped from taking his life if he wants to?" My reply was "yes I do, because during that moment of utter despair it's understandable that you may want to do this, but you never know what littlest thing there could have been, that you may not have been aware of at the time, and that littlest thing would have changed your mind and your outlook towards life." The patient accepted my reply and began to ponder on it. A couple of days later he acknowledged me and commented how dedicated I was to my job.

3. During my early years of practice as a Clinical Hypnotherapist a lady in her late thirties came to see me. She had been housebound and fearful for some months after having escaped from a violent relationship. In the end she became very depressed.

To protect her anonymity I shall call this lady Meredith. Meredith had got involved with a man who turned out to be very possessive and just wouldn't leave her alone. She managed to get away from him but he found her again and kept harassing her. Then she moved elsewhere but was very afraid to leave the house in case she was seen by him and it would start all over again.

Meredith had previously been a capable and independent woman. She had earned a living by decorating denim clothes that she bought cheaply from op shops and then sold the vamped up products at markets for a profit. But because of her fear and self-isolation she lost her self-esteem and gradually became more and more depressed.

She stopped doing what was previously successful for her. Meredith consented to treatment on the condition that she commit to three sessions and follow my instructions to the tee. I stipulated she could do this or she could leave right there and then and not pay a penny.

After the three sessions I recorded a tape and gave it to her to use as a booster when needed. Upon follow up Meredith said she was back to her old self again and when she started feeling down she would lie down and play the tape. She said when she listened to the tape she would "drift off to I don't know where" then come back feeling better.

So as you can see there is a solution to depression no matter what problem or obstacle comes your way. Sometimes you may need to seek outside help but there are plenty of ways in this book that you can use to help yourself.

When is Depression Normal?

Depression is normal after certain events in your life. In order of severity: Loss of parent, spouse or other loved one, loss of a friend, loss of employment, break up of a relationship. Illness, injury or catastrophic events can also bring on depression.

A period of grieving after any of these events, especially when someone has passed away is normal and even socially expected. Eventually you adapt to the new circumstances and continue with your life, though there can be periods of sadness when memories resurface.

You may have lost your job through downsizing or were looked over for promotion or you were dismissed. Yes these events can also bring on a period of depression. It is often because along with such changes in your life comes anger, disappointment, loss of self-esteem and more time to dwell on these things.

Then there's the reality of loss of income and how are you going to survive, and this is a real problem. Nevertheless the battle for survival can also help you because it motivates you to move on, to find another job, or to generate some income.

What Causes Depression?

Given the complexity of the body, brain and mind, single causes are difficult to isolate, therefore I have presented the following items for your consideration:

Genetics: Studies of twins have shown that depression can be inherited. The genetic risk of developing clinical depression is about 40%. However this is only a predisposition and the depression may not manifest.

Environmental: The remaining 60% is due to factors in the individual's own environment, whatever that may be: home environment, school environment, poverty are just a few examples.

Life Events: Depression is unlikely to occur without life events, but the risk of developing depression as a result of some such event is strongly genetically determined. It is unlikely that any one contributing gene will be identified.

Personality Characteristics: It may be that some of the genetic risk is associated with melancholic depression and, as well, to certain personality 'styles' that increase the chance of developing non-melancholic depression. There have been a number of reports of genes associated with particular personality characteristics. For example, genes have been identified that seem to be associated with novelty-seeking behavior, and others that are linked to high anxiety levels.

Biochemical: In normal brain function, neurotransmitters jump from one nerve cell to the next, with the signal being as strong in the second and subsequent cells as it was in the first. Neurotransmitters also need to be in balance. However, in people who are depressed, the mood regulating neurotransmitters fail to function normally, so that the signal is either depleted or disrupted before passing to the next nerve cell. In some cases there may be underproduction or depletion of certain neurotransmitters, especially serotonin. This view has recently been challenged by Dr Mercola. You will read about this in a later chapter.

Stress: It is important to recognize that nearly every individual can be stressed and depressed by certain events. Past and long-standing stresses (called distal stressors) can increase the chance of an individual developing depression in later years. The most clearly established past stressor is that of an uncaring parent or an abusive parent. The lack of parental care may result in the child developing a low self-esteem and thus being vulnerable to develop depression in adult life. The events that are most likely to 'trigger' depression are ones where the individual's self-esteem is put at risk, compromised or devalued. For most adults, self-esteem is closely linked to an intimate relationship as well as to other important areas, such as a job or career. Thus, the break-up of a relationship or a marriage or losing a job are very common triggers for depression.

Anxiety: It has been suggested that long term unresolved anxiety may result in depression. Indeed this could have been true in

Meredith's case, mentioned in a previous chapter, because Meredith would have been continually anxious that her former boyfriend would find her again.

Anger and/or frustration: Just like anxiety, anger or frustration if not resolved can turn inward and be very destructive. For example you are angry at your boss for the way he talks to you and frustrated because you feel powerless to do anything about it. 17 This anger and frustration may go on day after day during your working hours, often also affecting you at night and on your weekends. This can get you down, more and more. Eventually you begin to become angry and frustrated with yourself for not doing anything about it. You don't want to quit your job, because you may not get another and you don't want to confront your boss, for fear of losing your job. You've stuck yourself in a loop and it can seem hopeless. Depression due to anger and frustration towards oneself is in my opinion one of the most dangerous kind of depression because it can lead to self harm and in the extreme it can lead to suicide.

Social Comparison: Social comparison i.e. comparing yourself to your peers can have an impact on happiness. As a matter of fact social comparison is a major driver of unhappiness. This will be dealt with in the next chapter – Happiness V Depression.

But don't get too hung up on all these possible causes. What really matters now is what you do about your depressed state. Don't go back, move forward!

Happiness V Depression

Instead of studying depression, some bold researchers have taken the approach of starting from the opposite pole i.e. they are questioning why some people don't get depressed. What is it that differentiates those people from those that do get depressed? Why is it that some people can face the adverse situations that life presents them and come through without becoming depressed?

This research has revealed that people who are less susceptible to depression tend to rate more highly on scales of happiness, gratefulness and optimism. The science of positive psychology has emerged from these findings.

Positive psychology is an attempt to explain, codify and eventually design therapy around the idea that there are a series of personal beliefs and behaviors which increase psychological resilience to adversity and reduce the likelihood of developing mood disorders.

Great inroads have already been achieved in this field by Martin Seligman and Sonja Lyubormirsky. They have developed an immense and ever growing body of literature on positive psychology and designed tools which can be used by clinicians to implement these ideas.

An online experiment by Seligman and colleagues on a group of 411 mildly depressed individuals produced very positive results. The volunteers were engaged for seven days in one of five well-being enhancing activities that involved practicing gratitude, positive thinking, and focusing on one's strengths. The result was that they experienced a boost in well-being and a decline in depressive symptoms, and these benefits were maintained well after the experiment ended.

Two of the activities in particular: writing about three good things in your life and using your key strengths in a new way resulted in the most lasting improvement of depression. You shall learn how to do these in the next chapter.

Social comparison as a major driver of unhappiness:

If you have spent time with children you would know that the quickest way to make children unhappy is to provide just one child in a group with a benefit, toy or treat that the others do not receive. The child receiving the benefit becomes happier for a while but the happiness of the rest of the children in the group suddenly vanishes. Happiness in the rest of the group is easily replaced by anger and jealousy.

Even if they were previously happy with their lot, the act of comparison to the child that received something leads them to feel unhappy because they perceive themselves to be less fortunate than the others.

This has been referred to by some psychologists as "status anxiety" and volumes have been written on the topic. This unconscious mechanism can operate within us as adults unless we become aware of it.

When we compare ourselves to others, and believe they are happier than us or more capable or have higher status then, like the children, we can start to make ourselves unhappy.

A prime example of this is a friend of mine who is in his fifties. He told me about a new twenty three year old worker who joined the department. The new worker is at the beginning of a blossoming career, he already owns a house in a prime location, is out partying nearly every night and seems to live a life free of responsibility or obligation.

In contrast my friend sees his own career path as having hit a brick wall, he is stuck with a mortgage on a run-down property in a location he considers as inferior, he has hardly any energy to party, in short he is unhappy.

When you compare yourself to others or measure your emotional state on what you perceive outside of yourself, you are in danger of making yourself unhappy or depressed. The reality is that you can never be really sure how happy or unhappy another person is unless they tell you.

In most cases you can only see what the person is showing you, and most people are very good at hiding their inner self. So what do you do if you are feeling unhappy? Here are some happiness enhancing strategies you can use:

1. **Count your blessings**: I know you have heard this over and over again but what I mean is to actually feel and

express gratitude for what you have. If you don't know what you have, how about: you have the eyes to be reading this, you have the ability to read, and you have the equipment on which to read? Come on ... WAKE UP!

2. **Cultivate Optimism**: Yes, I said cultivate. This is like cultivating a field to grow a crop. It takes time, but taking the time to cultivate it will ensure an excellent crop. Once you have cultivated optimism it will be easier to remain optimistic. Therefore start to imagine, think about and plan the best possible future for yourself and practice to look on the bright side of every situation.

3. **Avoid over-thinking and social comparison**: Cut down how often you dwell on your problems and compare yourself to others. Use distraction: read a book, go for a walk, watch a movie or think about something else instead.

4. **Practice acts of kindness**: Do good things for others, friends or strangers, anonymously or directly, spontaneous or planned.

5. **Nurture relationships**: Choose a relationship in need of strengthening and put time and energy into healing, cultivating, affirming and enjoying it.

6. **Do more of the activities that you enjoy and that absorb your attention**: Increase the number of experiences in which you 'lose' yourself.

7. **Replay and savour life's joys**: Take delight in, and go over, life's momentary pleasures and wonders – through thinking, writing, drawing or sharing with others. 8. Commit to your goals: Pick one, two or three significant goals that

are meaningful to you and devote time and effort to pursuing them.

8. **Develop strategies for coping**: Practice ways to endure or surmount stress, hardship or trauma.

9. **Learn to forgive**: Keep a journal or write a letter in which you work on letting go of anger and resentment towards one or more individuals who have hurt you or wronged you.

10. **Practice religion and spirituality**: Many people find happiness when they become more involved in their church, temple or mosque. Or you could read spiritually oriented books or dedicate more time to spirituality in whatever form resonates with you.

11. **Take care of your mind and body**: Engage in physical activity, eat healthy food, meditate, smile and laugh.

In the next chapter you will go through the main steps that brought huge results in the study done by Martin Seligman and his colleagues. They are evidence based techniques that will prove just as effective for you.

Expressing Gratitude
and Using Your Strengths

I n the previous chapter you learned twelve happiness enhancing strategies you can use if you are feeling unhappy. In this chapter you will learn how to use the two principal strategies that achieved the highest results in the experiment by Seligman and his colleagues. Write about three good things in your life and use your key strengths. These are proven strategies that will lift you up from your depressive state.

1.**Write about three good things in your life**: This is basically about gratitude, it is a gratitude exercise. It is suggested you keep a journal. Each day write at least three good things that are in your life, no matter how trivial they seem to you because even if they seem trivial to you, there would be some people in the world that are lacking those things. It's a good idea to use the journal in the morning and in the evening before bed.

In the evening you write about the good things that happened during the day up to the time you went to bed. The idea is that you set yourself up with a positive outlook for the day and then for a good sleep at night. I shall write three examples to get you started, then you write your own.

Monday am:

The sunrise this morning is breathtaking

I enjoyed a lovely cup of coffee

The new breakfast cereal was delicious

Monday pm:

I finished my work on time today

The sandwich I had for lunch was nice

Dinner tonight was excellent

Continue in a similar manner for each day of the week and do this for at least two weeks. More if you wish.

2. **Use your key strengths**:

Everyone has strengths and weaknesses. The trouble is that when we are in a depressed state we tend to focus on our weaknesses instead of our strengths.

Here are some examples of strengths you may have and how to use them, Fill the rest of the table with your strengths and add more if you need:

STRENGTH	HOW I CAN USE IT
I am a kind person	I express my kindness by doing volunteer work for a charitable organization
I am artistic	I create some artworks and arrange to exhibit them, either on my own or in a group exhibition
I am a wonder-ful mother	I can give my children a good example by lifting myself above the depression for my children's sake

So these are the two main techniques that were proven to have achieved results with the majority of students who took part in the study. A third technique was also tested but not discussed and that was "turn your negative thoughts into positive thoughts." This does not mean that it has to be the exact opposite of the negative thought but it has to be a statement that will be at least a step toward the positive.

This can be done in three phases:

1. Write down the negative thought
2. Write down the positive thought that you want in its place
3. Fill in the transition phase, what you need to do to change the thought

Here is an example:

Negative thought: *I am not smart*

Positive thought: *I am smarter than I believe*

Transition Phase: *I pick an interest in my life that I like and become very knowledgeable about it*

And another example:

Negative thought: *I'll never get out of debt*

Positive thought: *I manage my money better so that I become debt free*

Transition Phase - *I design a budget that will allow for steady regular repayment of debt until I am debt free. If I can't do the budget myself I shall ask someone to do it with me*

Now fill in the table with your own thoughts. Remember first write the negative thought, then the positive thought. The transition phase will come to mind of its own accord

Negative Thought	Transition Phase	Positive Thought
I'm not smart		I am smarter than I believe
I'll never get out of debt		I manage my money better so that I become debt free

I can tell you about a method I used to lift myself out of a period of depression and shattered self esteem. It happened during my second year at university, I can testify that this technique really worked because I achieved the desired result.

It so happened that during my second year an ex-girlfriend came back after eighteen months overseas in another relationship. Needless to say I couldn't help giving in to a night of intimacy because I had been very much in love with her.

Then she took up with another man I knew whom she met via another friend of mine. I felt betrayed, my self esteem was shattered and I fell into depression again. The depression affected my concentration and focus with my university work and as a result I failed most of my subjects that year.

I was asked to see the Dean and had to justify why I should be allowed to continue my studies. I explained to him what had happened and he suggested I could take a year's leave from the course and come back after I had recovered. I decided against this alternative and assured the Dean that I would be OK. Needless to say I was really down after that meeting but determined to do something about it.

On my way home I stopped at a park and sat on a flat elevated rock just gazing at nothing in particular when I remembered having read somewhere about visualization.

Visualization

As you probably know, visualization is a useful tool that can be used to make things happen for you. Take this example and modify it for your own use when you think it will help. This is what I did:

1. I visualized the report with the failed exam results. They show up as 'F' against each subject

2. I then visualized each 'F' disappearing

3. Finally I replaced each 'F' with a 'P' while at the same time bringing on good feelings about the new results.

The next day I made an appointment to see a student counselor. During our session I told him about my fails saying I know I'm not stupid but I have trouble passing exams. The counselor briefed me on how most students passed their exams and how some got even better results. I decided to put in the effort to follow all his suggestions. The following year I passed all subjects and some with Credits and one Distinction.

Before I leave this topic I want to tell you more about visualization. The visual you get does not have to be crystal clear. Give it your best effort of course but not everyone has the same capacity for it. If you want to practice, close your eyes and try to visualize something familiar, say, an apple. When you can visualize it clearly enough, move on to your particular goal.

Can Loneliness Lead to Depression?

There was a time in my life when I was fairly free. I had a steady job that occupied me during the day. I had a good motor vehicle to get me around, and I was very sociable. My lifestyle consisted of going to work during the day and most evenings I would either go out to hear live music or visit friends.

In those days it was acceptable to go knock on a friend's door, check if they're busy and just pop in for a visit. This was because not everyone had a telephone and cell phones didn't even exist. But something else was happening around me; some older friends were getting married and moving away but that was OK, I made new friends.

The new friends were intelligent and fun, they had parties and I had parties. We went out together to pubs, movies and harbor cruises. Even just hanging at their place was fun.

It was all very wonderful! There was one basic difference between them and me. They were university students and I wasn't. One was studying to be a medical doctor; the others were training to be teachers.

During the time when we were having fun, they were on vacation. When vacation was over they went back to their usual routine of study, assignments and exams. So going around in the evenings just to hang out was not convenient for them anymore.

I recall one night in particular when I went and knocked on their door. Alex answered asking "what's up?" I replied that nothing was up and that I came around to visit because I was lonely. Alex replied "sorry I'm busy, I've some assignments due."

I said all right then turned around and walked away. I was hurting. The logical part of my mind understood that Alex did have to get on with his work but at an emotional level there was still the hurt of feeling rejected. What was worse was that at a subconscious level the rejection became generalized. I became fearful to go visit other people in case I was "rejected".

As illogical as it may seem the loneliness worsened and started me down into one of my spirals of depression. So can loneliness lead to depression? It did for me. Since then there were times I was lonely even when I was with my girlfriend

Fortunately this is not the case for everyone. There are peo-ple who are happier on their own. There are also people who have escaped toxic relationships and find peace and solace by themselves. There are those who seek the solitude of a retreat in order to "sort themselves out". And finally there are people who like being by themselves and loneliness has never been an issue.

There is a difference between loneliness and solitude. So if you believe you like solitude, that's fine. If you are lonely and feel you would like some company, go places or seek out people who are likely to be good company for you. Maybe this is not so easy to do in the current pandemic but surely this too will come to pass.

Types of Treatment for Depression

Medical Treatment

See your doctor about Medical Treatment. Your doctor may prescribe some medication or refer you to a Mental Health Specialist for further treatment. Mental Health Specialists (psychiatrists) are trained to prescribe certain drugs and usually provide psychotherapy.

The three groups of drugs most likely to be used for depression are antidepressants, tranquilizers and anti-manic drugs or mood stabilizers.

There are a large number of antidepressants. They have a role in many types of depression and vary in their effectiveness across the more biological depressive conditions. New drugs are being developed all the time.

Medications can have harmful effects and therefore should only be used in extreme circumstances and strictly under professional advice. See the article by Dr Mercola below.*

Selective Serotonin Reuptake Inhibitors (SSRIs), Tricyclics (TCAs) and Irreversible Monoamine Oxidase Inhibitors (MAOIs) are three common classes of antidepressants. The latter two are characterized by broader actions. They each work in different ways and have different applications.

Clinicians at the Black Dog Institute firmly believe that it is important to find the right antidepressant as different antidepressants produce different effects and result in different people. If the first antidepressant does not work, it is sensible to move to a different kind of antidepressant. For the biological depressive disorders, more broad action antidepressants are usually more effective.

A well-informed health professional should be able to use assessment and their understanding of the person to determine the type of depression and its likely causes. The health professional can then identify the medication most likely to benefit or decide to not recommend medication at all. The latter decision is just as important.

Tranquilizers can be classified as 'minor' or 'major' tranquilizers. Minor tranquilizers (typically benzodiazepines) are not helpful in depression; they are addictive and can make the depression worse. Major tranquilizers are very useful in people with a psychotic or melancholic depression where the person is not being helped by other medications.

'Antimanic' drugs or 'mood stabilizers' are of great importance in Bipolar Disorder. Their use in treating mania makes them 'anti-manic', while their ability to reduce the severity and frequency of mood swings makes them 'mood stabilizers'. Lithium, valproate and carbamazepine are the most common mood stabilizers.

It is important to remember that the antidepressants and mood stabilizers are often necessary both to treat the depression that is occurring now, and to make a relapse in the future less likely. Consequently, people may need to continue taking medication for some time after they are better.

Medication should be used only under professional advice and professional monitoring. This article written by Dr Mercola a few years ago warns about the pitfalls and dangers of medication.

Social Anxiety Disorder Linked to High Serotonin Levels, Throwing Treatment with SSRIs into Serious Question

"Depression and other mental health problems are at epidemic levels judging by the number of antidepressants prescribed each year.

According to CDC data, one in twenty Americans over the age of twelve report some form of depression, and eleven percent of the US population over the age of twelve is on antidepressant medication. This despite overwhelming evidence showing that antidepressants do not work as advertised.

"At best, antidepressants are comparable to placebos," says Dr Mercola, "at worst they can cause devastating side effects, including deterioration into more serious mental illness, and suicidal or homicidal tendencies."

Virtually all of the school and mass shooters, for example, have been on antidepressants. Antidepressants are also prescribed to pregnant women, which can have serious repercussions for the child.

Research shows boys with autism are three times more likely to have been exposed to antidepressants known as selective serotonin reuptake inhibitors (SSRIs) in utero than non-autistic boys. Those whose mothers used SSRIs during the first trimester were found to be at greatest risk.

Recent research into the mechanisms driving anxiety and social phobias now turn conventional drug treatment with SSRIs on its ear.

Turns out these mental health problems are not due to low serotonin levels as previously thought. They're linked to high levels! If these findings are taken as seriously as they should be, the mental health field is in for a major overhaul.

The Low Serotonin Theory Was Never Proven True, Yet Spawned a Booming Market of SSRIs

Prozac was released in 1987 in the US, giving rise to an entire new antidepressant therapy class known as selective serotonin reuptake inhibitors (SSRIs). Some of the most popular ones include:

- Paxil (fluoxetine)
- Celexa (citalopram)
- Zoloft (sertraline)
- Paxil (paroxetine)
- Lexapro (escitalopram)

SSRIs work by preventing the reuptake (movement back into the nerve endings) of the neurotransmitter serotonin. This makes more serotonin available for use in your brain, which is thought to improve your mood.

Most people have heard of the "chemical imbalance" theory, which states that depression and anxiety disorders are due to low serotonin levels. Most believe this theory to be true. But the theory was just that—a theory. It sounds scientific, but there was actually no hard evidence behind it.

As explained by investigative health journalist Robert Whitaker, in 1983 the National Institutes of Mental Health (NIMH) investigated whether or not depressed individuals had low serotonin. At that time, they concluded there was no evidence that there is anything wrong in the serotonergic system of depressed patients.

Research published in 2009 added further evidence to the pile indicating the low serotonin idea was incorrect, as they found strong indications that depression actually begins further up in the chain of events in the brain. Essentially, the medications have been focusing on the effect, not the cause.

Drug companies kept running with the low serotonin theory though, as it justifies the aggressive use of antidepressants to correct this alleged "imbalance." Now, Swedish research really throws the justification for using SSRIs to treat anxiety disorders into question.

Anxiety Linked to High Serotonin Levels, Making SSRIs a Questionable Remedy

More than 25 million Americans report suffering from social anxiety disorder, which makes them feel embarrassed or severely uncomfortable in public situations.

As with depression, low serotonin has been the prevailing theory for explaining social anxiety, and hence SSRIs are typically prescribed for this disorder. (Other commonly prescribed anti-anxiety drugs include benzodiazepines, such as Ativan, Xanax, and Valium.

These are also associated with serious risks, including memory loss, hip fractures, and addiction. Among women who take SSRI's to counter symptoms of menopause, the drugs can significantly elevate their risk of bone fractures, and this risk lingers for several years.

One recent study found that, compared to women treated with H2 antagonists or proton pump inhibitors (indigestion drugs), SSRI's raised bone fracture rates by 76 percent in one year. After two years of treatment, the fracture rate was 73 percent higher. People who take these drugs are also nearly four times more likely to die prematurely than people who don't, and also have a 35 percent greater risk of cancer.

As reported by Medical Daily:

[Dr. Tomas] Furmark and Dr. Mats Fredrikson, another professor of psychology at Uppsala University, questioned the underlying hypothesis of treating patients with SSRIs: What molecular role, exactly, does serotonin play in social phobia? To discover the truth, they used brain scanning technology, PET scans, to measure serotonin in the brains of volunteers with social phobia.

Communication within the brain works like this: Nerve cells release serotonin into the space between nerve cells. Then, serotonin attaches itself to receptor cells. Following this, serotonin is released from the receptor and returns to the original cell.

The researchers discovered patients with social phobia were producing too much serotonin in the amygdala. This brain region, tucked deep inside our skulls, is the seat of our most primitive emotions, including fear. The more serotonin produced in this area, then, the more anxious people feel in social situations."

Previous studies have revealed that increased nerve activity in the amygdala is part of the underlying mechanism that produces anxiety. Basically, those with social phobia have an overactive fear center. These new findings provide additional information, suggesting increased serotonin production in the brain may be part of this mechanism.

Either way, when it comes to treating this anxiety disorder, increasing serotonin in your brain with an SSRI will not soothe your anxiety. It will increase it, making SSRIs a questionable treatment option.

Fermented Foods May Help Social Anxiety Disorder, Study Finds

The impact of your gut microbiome on your brain function has been confirmed by a number of studies, and research is moving rather swiftly in this area. One of the reasons for why the bacterial makeup of your gut would have an influence on your mental and emotional health relates to the fact that your gut actually works much like a second brain.

Your central nervous system (composed of your brain and spinal cord) and your enteric nervous system (the intrinsic nervous system of your gastrointestinal tract) are created from identical tissue during fetal development. One part turns into your central nervous system while the other develops into your enteric nervous system. These two systems are connected via the vagus nerve, the tenth cranial nerve that runs from your brain stem down to your abdomen.

It is now well established that the vagus nerve is the primary route your gut bacteria use to transmit information to your brain. Even more interesting, serotonin is produced in your gut as well as your brain, by specific bacteria. In fact, the greatest concentration of serotonin is found in your intestines, not your brain.

It's not so surprising then that researchers keep finding positive correlations between gut health and improved mental health. Most recently, researchers found that fermented foods and drinks helped curb social anxiety disorder in young adults. The study,12,13 published in Psychiatry Research, involved 710 psychology students at the College of William and Mary.

The participants filled out questionnaires rating their level of worry and anxiety, and documented their fermented food consumption over the past 30 days. Other factors such as healthy diet and exercise were also addressed. Among those who rated themselves as having a high degree of neurotic feelings, eating more fermented foods was linked to fewer symptoms of social anxiety. Meaning, the relationship between fermented foods and decreased social anxiety was strongest among those who tended to be more neurotic.

Key Factors to Overcoming Anxiety and/or Depression Without Drugs

It's important to realize that your diet and general lifestyle are foundational factors that must be optimized if you want to resolve mental health problems such as depression or anxiety, because your body and mind are so closely interrelated. Compelling research demonstrates just how interconnected your mental health is with your gastrointestinal health for example. While many think of their brain as the organ in charge of their mental health, your gut may actually play a far more significant role. The drug treatments available today for depression are no better than they were 50 years ago.

Clearly, we need a new approach, and your diet is an obvious place to start. Research tells us that the composition of your gut flora not only affects your physical health, but also has a significant impact on your brain function and mental state, and your gut microbiome can be quickly impacted by dietary changes—for better or worse.

Research has also revealed there are a number of other safe effective ways to address depression and anxiety that do not involve hazardous drugs. So, if you suffer from an anxiety or depression-related disorder, please consider addressing the following diet and lifestyle factors before you resort to drugs:

1. ***Dramatically decrease your consumption of processed foods, sugar (particularly fructose), grains, and GMOs (Genetically Modified Organisms.)***

High sugar and starchy carbohydrates lead to excessive insulin release, which can result in falling blood sugar levels, or hypoglycemia. In turn, hypoglycemia causes your brain to secrete glutamate in levels that can cause agitation, depression, anger, anxiety, and panic attacks. Additionally, sugar fans the flames of inflammation in your body. In addition to being high in sugar and grains, processed foods also contain a variety of additives that can affect your brain function and mental state, especially MSG, and artificial sweeteners such as aspartame.

There's a great book on this subject, The Sugar Blues, written by William Dufty more than 30 years ago, that delves into the topic of sugar and mental health in great detail. Recent research also shows that glyphosate, which is used in large quantities on genetically engineered (GE) crops like corn, soy, and sugar beets, limits your body's ability to detoxify foreign chemical compounds. As a result, the damaging effects of those toxins are magnified, potentially resulting in a wide variety of diseases, including brain disorders that have both psychological and behavioral effects.

Increase consumption of traditionally fermented and cultured foods

Reducing gut inflammation is imperative when addressing mental health issues,14 so optimizing your gut flora is a critical piece. To promote healthy gut flora, increase your consumption of probiotic foods, such as fermented vegetables, kimchee, natto, kefir, and others.

Get adequate vitamin B12

Vitamin B12 deficiency can contribute to depression and affects one in four people.

Optimize your vitamin D levels

Vitamin D is very important for your mood. In one study, people with the lowest levels of vitamin D were found to be 11 times more prone to depression than those who had normal levels.15 Remember, SAD (Seasonal Affective Disorder) is a type of depression that we know is related to sunshine deficiency, so it would make sense that the perfect way to optimize your vitamin D is through sun exposure or a tanning bed. If neither are available, an oral vitamin D3 supplement is highly advisable. Just remember to also increase your vitamin K2 when taking oral vitamin D.

Get plenty of animal-based omega-3 fats

Your brain is 60 percent fat, and DHA, an animal-based omega-3 fat, along with EPA, is crucial for good brain function and mental health.16 Research has shown a 20 percent reduction in anxiety among medical students taking omega-3s.

Unfortunately, most people don't get enough from diet alone, so make sure you take high-quality omega-3 fat, such as krill oil. Dr. Stoll, a Harvard psychiatrist, was one of the early leaders in compiling the evidence supporting the use of animal based omega-3 fats for the treatment of depression. He wrote an excellent book that details his experience in this area called "The Omega-3 Connection."

Evaluate your salt intake

Sodium deficiency actually creates symptoms that are very much like those of depression. Make sure you do NOT use processed salt (regular table salt), however. You'll want to use an all natural, unprocessed salt like Himalayan salt, which contains more than 80 different micronutrients.

Get adequate daily exercise

Exercise is one of the most effective strategies for preventing and overcoming depression. Studies have shown there is a strong correlation between improved mood and aerobic capacity. So there's a growing acceptance that the mind-body connection is very real, and that maintaining good physical health can significantly lower your risk of developing depression in the first place.

Exercising creates new GABA-producing neurons that help induce a natural state of calm. It also boosts your levels of serotonin, dopamine, and norepinephrine, which help buffer the effects of stress.

Get enough sleep

You can have the best diet and exercise program possible but if you aren't sleeping well you can easily become depressed. Sleep and depression are so intimately linked that a sleep disorder is actually part of the definition of the symptom complex that gives the label depression.

Tapping Your Anxiety Away

Energy Psychology Techniques such as Emotional Freedom Technique (EFT) are very effective for reducing anxiety by correcting the bioelectrical short-circuiting that causes your body's reactions—without adverse effects. You can think of EFT as a tool for "reprogramming" your circuitry, and it works on both real and imagined stressors.

EFT is a form of psychological acupressure, based on the same energy meridians used in traditional acupuncture for more than 5,000 years to treat physical and emotional ailments, but without the invasiveness of needles. Following a 2012 review in the American Psychological Association's journal Review of General

Psychology, EFT is moving closer to meeting the criteria for an "evidence-based treatment." *

Recent research has shown that EFT significantly increases positive emotions, such as hope and enjoyment, and decreases negative emotional states, including anxiety. EFT is particularly powerful for treating stress and anxiety because it specifically targets your amygdala and hippocampus, which are the parts of your brain that help you decide whether or not something is a threat. If you recall NIMH's explanation about how your amygdala and hippocampus are involved in anxiety disorders, you can see why tapping is such a powerful tool. EFT has also been shown to lower cortisol levels.

Although you can learn the basics of EFT on your own, if you or your child has a serious anxiety disorder, I highly recommend that you consult a qualified EFT practitioner. For serious or complex issues you need a qualified health care professional that is trained in EFT to help guide you through the process, as it typically takes years of training to develop the skill to tap on and relieve deep-seated, significant issues.

There are situations where SSRIs may be warranted, but on the whole, these mind and body-numbing drugs are grossly over-used. I'd be willing to bet a majority of people taking them are not appropriate candidates, and would fare much better were they to address the basic, core issues relating to their general lifestyle and health. This includes proper diet, sleep, exercise, and employing effective tools for stress relief.

Exposure to the outdoors, such as walking barefoot through a grassy field and getting appropriate amounts of sun exposure, also should not be underestimated. If you're suffering from emotional or physical pain, I encourage you to peruse my inventory of tens of thousands of articles, which address these issues and offer a multitude of safe and effective alternatives."

*Latest research has shown EFT to be an "evidence-based treatment."

Psychological Treatment

There is a wide range of psychological treatments for depression. Some of the main ones are:

- Cognitive Behavior Therapy (CBT)

- Interpersonal Therapy (IPT)

- Acceptance Commitment Therapy (ACT)

- Psychotherapies

- Counseling

- Narrative Therapy

- Hypnotherapy

Psychological treatments provide either an alternative to medication or work alongside medication. As always, a thorough assessment of the person should be carried out in order to decide on the best set of approaches.

Cognitive Behavior Therapy (CBT) People suffering from depression - particularly 'non-melancholic depression' - will often have an ongoing negative view about themselves and the world around them.This negative way of thinking is often not confined to depression, but is an ongoing part of how they think about life.

Many or all of their experiences are distorted through a negative filter and their thinking patterns become so entrenched that they don't even notice the errors of judgment caused by thinking irrationally.

CBT aims to show people how their thinking affects their mood and to teach them to think in a less negative way about life and themselves. It is based on the understanding that thinking negatively is a habit, and, like any other bad habit, it can be broken.

CBT is conducted by trained therapists either in one-on-one therapy sessions or in small groups. 'Homework' may also be assigned between sessions. Between six and 10 sessions can be required but the number will vary from person to person.

CBT is one of the more effective treatments available for depression.

Mindfulness Based Cognitive Therapy (MBCT) You will find information about this in a later chapter.

Interpersonal Therapy (IPT) The causes of depression, or our vulnerabilities to developing depression, can often be traced to aspects of social functioning (work, relationships, and social roles) and personality.

Therefore, the underlying assumption of interpersonal therapy is that depression and interpersonal problems are interrelated.

The goal of interpersonal therapy is to understand how these factors are operating in the person's current life situation leading them to become depressed and putting them at risk of future depression. Usually twelve to sixteen sessions of IPT will be required.

Acceptance Commitment Therapy (ACT) ACT is a type of CBT. It is thought to work by helping people to stop avoiding difficult experiences, especially by "over thinking" these experiences. Over thinking occurs when people focus on the "verbal commentary" in their mind rather than the experiences themselves.

ACT encourages people to accept their reactions and to experience them without trying to change them. Once the people have done this, they are then encouraged to choose a way to respond to situations that is consistent with their values, and to put those choices into action.

Psychotherapies Psychotherapy is an extended treatment (months to years) in which a relationship is developed between the therapist and the patient. The relationship is then used to explore aspects of the person's experience in great depth. Understanding the link between past and present and the supportive relationship between therapist and patient are thought to resolve the depression and make the person less vulnerable to becoming depressed again.

Counseling Counseling encompasses a broad set of approaches and skills that aim to help an individual explore problems and preferred scenarios. Counseling helps people with long-standing problems in the family or at work, as well as sudden major problems (crisis counseling).

Narrative Therapy (NT) Narrative Therapy is a form of counseling based on understanding the 'stories' that people use to describe their lives. The therapist listens to how people describe their problems as stories and helps the person to consider how the stories may restrict them from overcoming their present difficulties

NT sees problems as being separate from people and assists the individual to recognize the range of skills, beliefs and abilities that they already have (but may not recognize) and that they can apply to the problems in their lives.

Narrative Therapy differs from many therapies in that it puts a major emphasis on identifying people's strengths, highlighting evidence of mastering problems in the past. It seeks to build on people's resilience rather than focus on their negative experiences.

Hypnotherapy The use of Hypnotherapy in treatment of depression has recently come under focus thanks to the investigations by Dr Ernest Rossi, a Clinical Psychologist and Hypnotherapist.

Dr Rossi has had a passionate interest in Psychosocial Genomics since the early seventies. The unravelling of the human genome and the mapping of human genes has broadened this area of research.

The introduction of microarray analysis has now made it possible to analyze changes in gene expression before and after a therapy. Experimentation by Dr Rossi has proved that changes in gene expression do occur after hypnosis.

Another pioneer in the use of Hypnotherapy for depression is Dr Michael Yapko. Dr Yapko has broken down into major categories the factors that contribute to the maintenance of depression and has developed therapy that addresses each of those factors, resulting in a complete system of treatment of depression using Hypnotherapy.

Finally a recent study has shown that when depression is a component of physical illness, better recovery is achieved when Hypnotherapy is used as part of the treatment.

Complementary Therapies

This group covers a wide range of modalities. I have learnt to not dismiss anything offered within this range because no matter how ridiculous or "way out" it may seem, there is always someone who benefits from it. In this book I will focus on the better known complementary therapies.

Acupuncture

Eight small studies were conducted with depressed people that compared acupuncture with "sham" acupuncture (i.e. very shallow insertion of needles with no stimulation). The number of sessions varied between 10 and 30. The pooling together of results from the eight studies found that acupuncture reduced depression symptoms.

How does it work?

Traditional Chinese Medicine (TCM) believes it works by correcting the flow of energy (chi) in the body. Western Medicine believes it may stimulate nerves which results in the release of serotonin and norepinephrine. It is because these neurotransmitters are thought to be lacking in people suffering depression.

Dance and Movement Therapy (DMT)

DMT combines expressive dancing with more usual psychological therapy approaches to depression, such as discussion of a person's life difficulties.

A DMT session usually starts with a warm up then a period of expressive dancing or movement. This is followed by a discussion of the client's feelings and thoughts about the experience and how it relates to their life situation.

DMT appears to be a helpful treatment for depression when used with other established treatments rather than on its own.

Light Therapy

Light therapy is the best treatment for Seasonal Affective Disorder (SAD) and may also be useful for depression when used with anti-depressants. The best effect is obtained when exposure is 5,000 lux per hour.

It is important the correct kind of light is used and that you are not directly looking at the light. Mild side effects can occur; such as nausea, headache, jumpiness or jitteriness, and eye irritation.

Massage

Two studies on massage were carried out: one with depressed children and adolescents and one with depressed pregnant women. The studies compared massage with relaxation therapy.

The result was a short term improvement after one massage and longer term improvements with regular massages over days or weeks.

Negative Air Ionization

A negative air ionizer is a device that uses high voltage to electrically charge air particles. Breathing these negatively charged particles is thought to improve depression.

Alfred Bellanti

A study was carried out with adults who had been depressed for a long time. They were exposed to high density negative ionization one hour each day or to a placebo (low density ionization). Half of these people recovered compared to none who received the placebo.

Another study carried out with people suffering Seasonal Affective Disorder (SAD). This study also confirmed success with Ionization compared to placebo.

Relaxation Training

There are different types of relaxation training. The most common one teaches the person to relax by voluntary tensing and relaxing specific groups of muscles. Another type of relaxation training involves thinking of relaxing scenes or places.

Several small studies have been carried out. The pooling of results showed that relaxation training reduced depression more than no treatment, but not as effectively as psychological therapies.

Relaxation training can be learnt through a professional or with an MP3 or CD. Recorded instructions can be found for free on the internet.

Herbal, Homeopathic and Nutritional Supplements

Back in the days when I was depressed most doctors believed that Nutritional Supplements were totally unnecessary. The standard opinion was you get all the vitamins and supplements if you eat properly.

Nothing could be further from the truth! The fact that you are depressed itself indicates that there is something lacking. The mind and body cannot be separated otherwise your brain would keep working if your head was removed from your body.

Furthermore, agricultural practices these days are not geared to producing the most nutritious food. They are more concerned with size, quantity and appearance of the vegetables or fruit. Most of the soils in which the crops are grown have been depleted of nutrients.

Then there's the use of herbicides, insecticides and other sprays. Organically grown food is much better though usually more expensive.

Therefore it makes sense that if there is a deficiency in emotional and psychological functioning then there could be a nutritional deficiency as well.

Herbs: Mankind has used herbs for millions of years. The World Health Organization reports that 80% of the world population still uses herbs as a primary form of treatment.

The use of herbs for medicinal, religious, cultural or recreational reasons has been well documented and there is now much scientific evidence that supports the traditional use of many herbs.

Herbs are powerful agents and it is recommended you seek consultation with an experienced herbalist to determine which herb or mixture of herbs best suits your condition. The following list is provided for educational reasons only.

St John's Wort (Hypericum perforatum) this herb has been shown to relieve anxiety and mild depression.

Gotu Kola (Centella asiatica) – A brain tonic

Brahmi (Bacopa moniera) – Another brain tonic, it is calming and assists with learning and memory.

Gingko (Gingko biloba) – Stimulates blood circulation to the body peripherals and hence it brings more oxygen to the brain. It can have a revitalizing effect and improve memory and learning.

Winter Cherry (Withania somnifera) – Can be calming and help with sleep.

Ginseng – There are various forms of Ginseng. The most appropriate one to use would depend on your constitution and various other factors. Contra-indications: Large doses may cause depression, insomnia and nervous disorders. Do not combine with any herbal remedies containing iron, or with Indian or China tea.

Vervain (Verbena officinalis) – Used in the treatment of nervous complaints such as depression and with other remedies in skin complaints.

Rhodiola - Rhodiola rosea is an herb that's popular for its "adaptogenic" properties (reducing fatigue and exhaustion in prolonged stressful situations)

This is by no means a comprehensive list. You should consult a herbalist who can make a mixture of herbs more specific to your constitution and psychological condition.

Homeopathics

There are homeopathic remedies available for depression. Classical homeopaths can prescribe classical remedies. There is also a modern form of homeopathy that is a bridge between allopathic remedies and homeopathic remedies.

Nutritional supplements: A good vitamin B complex assists the nervous system.

5 HTP (5 - hydroxytryptophan) - can increase serotonin levels.

DHA (docosahexaenoic acid) – is found in fish oil. It is important to use fish oil with a high DHA: EPA ratio.

Herbs, homeopathics and nutritional supplements can be used alone or in combination. It is better to get professional advice to avoid unnecessary expenditure on misinformed choices.

It is best to start these treatments with detoxification. This will result in better and more effective absorption of herbs, homeopathics or nutritional supplements. Adequate detoxification can be obtained by taking Aloe Vera Juice.

A combination of Isotonix Vitamin D, B Complex OPC3 and CoQ10 has been known to help.

Emotional Freedom Technique (EFT)

EFT was already described in Dr Mercola's article so this description will be only brief. The therapy uses a combination of acupuncture with repetitive affirmations. Once the psychological issue has been discussed the therapist locates the appropriate meridians and points that are associated with that issue and asks the client to repeat certain affirmations either silently or verbally while the therapist taps the points repetitively.

A study in The Journal of Evidence-Based Integrative medicine reports that EFT demonstrates that its efficacy for anxiety, depression, phobias and PTSD is well-established.

How to Help Yourself

You are a unique human being. Most of the negative ideas or beliefs you hold about yourself have accumulated from your past and could be the result of someone else's input e.g. derogatory remarks from parents, teachers or other authority figures and/or from your reaction to life events.

Then there are the expectations, usually from parents. Expectations are what they'd like us to achieve. We may achieve the expectations, well and good.

What usually happens is that our parents' expectations are unconsciously internalized by us. Thus they can seem to be our expectations. And if they are not in accordance with our own desires, they can set up a situation of inner conflict.

If we don't measure up to the expectations then our self-esteem can suffer, giving fertile ground for depression.

The subconscious mind operates at a child-like level and can take any negative input and turn it into its own belief. Not only that, but it can seek out proof and present it to your conscious mind to corroborate those beliefs and thereby reinforce them.

You are not your past. You are no longer your past. You are the present and the future. The first step to relieving your depression is to unburden yourself from your past. Sure, we have all done things we are not proud of, we have all made mistakes. You undo what can be undone and forget the rest.

The process of undoing is a positive step toward future happiness. What you cannot undo, just forget it! Let it go! It is unnecessary baggage. It just blocks your way to finding the happiness you truly deserve.

You deserve happiness, all human beings deserve happiness. By believing and buying into your past you create more unhappiness. Therefore you must believe that your depression is now a thing of the past.

As you read this you must agree; you must believe your depression now belongs in the past. It is no longer in your present and no longer a part of your future.

Make a decision that your depression is a thing of the past. Leave it behind now! Belief is the key, even if you trick yourself into believing it.

I vividly remember a day not so long ago when again, I thought I was slipping into another phase of depression. I asked myself "how do I know that what I am feeling is depression?" "How do I know it is depression and not a normal way to feel or just my way of feeling?"

My self-questioning gave me the solution. I told myself to accept that what I was feeling was a normal state. So rather than perceive it as depression and let it keep me down, I accepted it as a normal state and decided to just carry on. It worked! Now every time I think or feel that I'm depressed, I know it's not really true, and I know it won't last!

One of the worst things you can do is to do nothing, and that's what I had done many, many years ago. When I was depressed, friends and parents used to ask me "why don't you do something?" Find a hobby; go to a movie, just do anything to occupy your time and you'll feel better.

I thought they missed the point. My point was that if I was ok then I shouldn't need to be doing something. It seemed like a rational way of thinking at the time. I really believed that if I was feeling ok then I shouldn't need to be doing something in order to feel better.

I didn't know enough then, I was not doing anything about my depression because I believed it needed to be cured for me and not by me. If I did know I could have done something about it myself instead of being stuck in the depressive state!

I thought that if I could feel good then feeling good would be enough of itself, and it seemed rational to think that way. Therefore I rejected comments, advice and recommendations. I didn't feel good and that was it!

Looking back I now realize how wrong I was back then. Life is all about action, achievement, relationships, following interests, experiencing highs and lows, and having interaction with other people.

It's especially about taking action to get out of your depression. That is easy for me to say now. It wasn't so easy back then. That is why I am sharing and making this point with you. I want to give you the benefit and the wisdom of my experience.

It is from these things that we get our feelings of accomplishment, our joy, our laughter. Not by isolation and withdrawing from activity and interaction with others.

By reading up to here you will have already gained a lot of knowledge that will help you. In the rest of this chapter I will cover other techniques that you can use to help yourself more; starting from the easiest and least invasive leading up to the more drastic kind of help available should you ever need it.

Exercise - Yes, having the motivation to exercise when you are depressed may seem a bit unrealistic. Nearly everyone I have spoken to has experienced supreme difficulty exercising whilst depressed.

Therefore even if exercising seems supremely difficult for you, it is not impossible! This is a treatment strategy that is accessible to everyone. And it's free!

If you do find motivation supremely difficult ask a friend or relative to push you or motivate you. It's for your own good and you will feel better in the long run! Give it a go for at least ten days. There will be an improvement!

The benefit of exercise is that exercise produces endorphins. Endorphins are your body's natural "feel good" chemicals. Unless your neurochemistry is really out of balance, a relatively short period of exercise will release your endorphins.

No one I have come across ever reported feeling worse after a walk. Dr Andrea Dunn recommends committing to exercising each day. In the beginning you may only walk for 10 minutes at a time.

Expose yourself to a little sunlight every day - Lack of sunlight can make depression worse. Make sure you're getting enough. Take a short walk outdoors, have your coffee outside, enjoy an al fresco meal, people-watch on a park bench, or sit out in the garden.

If you aim to increase the walking time by 10 minutes each week, you'll be walking the recommended 30 minutes per day by the third week.

If you're really pushed for time, three periods of 10 minutes exercise per day can have a similar effect as a 30 minute block.

A 2001 study by the Duke University in North Carolina found that exercise is a more effective treatment for depression than antidepressants, with fewer relapses and a higher recovery rate.

Furthermore the study likewise found patients who completed 30 minutes of brisk exercise at least three times a week had a significantly lower incidence of relapse when compared to people on drug treatment alone and people on the exercise plus drug treatment.

Only 8 percent of patients in the exercise group had their depression return, compared to 38 percent who had drug treatment only and compared to thirty one percent who had the exercise plus the drug.

Dr Andrea Dunn's study published in the January 2005 *American Journal of Preventative Medicine* found that the scores for the *Hamilton Rating Scale for Depression* were reduced by 47percent for those who did the equivalent of 35 minutes walking, five days per week. That means a 47percent reduction in depression state or feeling 47percent improved. Good whichever way you look at it.

Another study, conducted at the Cooper Research Institute in Dallas Texas, shows that as little as three hours of regular exercise a week reduces the symptoms of mild to moderate depression as effectively as Prozac and other antidepressants.

Of course walking is not the only exercise that will yield results. Swimming, running, zumba, cycling, aerobics, dancing, jazzercise, rowing, rollerblading, any exercise will be beneficial.

Aerobic exercise in particular, improves blood flow and oxygen to the brain. It has the added benefit of releasing endorphins (natural feel-good chemicals) into the body.

The message is clear: Start moving! Exercise in itself has benefits for people with depression. It can raise your serotonin levels and unlike medication, there are no detrimental side effects.

Some Quick Suggestions

If you scored within mild to moderate depression in your self-test then ask yourself "what can I do to bring this depression back one notch?" Whatever slightest thing; it could be cleaning out a drawer, going for a walk, going to a movie, calling a friend, anything. You'll understand why.

Often when we are depressed, we associate our surroundings with a depressed state. Staying in that environment or surroundings can keep you depressed unless you get out or do something within those surroundings that will take your focus away from your depression.

Doing something else,for example going for a long walk or to a movie gets you out of those surroundings, gives you different scenery, refreshes your spirit and can give you a lift or a fresher perspective no matter how slight.

Even within your surroundings, if you focus on something like cleaning out your drawer, it takes your attention off the depression and focuses it outside of yourself on to the task. And while you focus on the task, the focus on the surroundings diminishes.

When you complete the task it brings a feeling of satisfaction. The feeling of satisfaction can improve your mood. You bring this depression back one notch and the surroundings then seem less depressing.

In turn, the feeling of accomplishment then motivates you to complete another task: another drawer perhaps, a wardrobe. It brings the depression back another notch, or two.

Eventually the whole room is done and you can imagine the satisfaction that comes with having accomplished that! You then return to your surroundings in a better state, and the surroundings take on a different light. They are not as oppressive as before.

When your activity moves you back from say, a 7 to a 5 or 4, there is a marked improvement, and your outlook will become brighter. With your brighter outlook you will then think of other things you can do. Even your thinking will change and you can think about other ways to further improve your state.

Nutrition

There are two main nutritional concerns that can surface during depression. One is that there is no motivation to shop and to prepare healthy meals. Therefore you go hungry or just eat junk!

Some people in a depressed state eat more than usual, and they are more likely to eat junk! I once knew a woman who would eat lots of pizza when she was depressed; not just any pizza, it had to be Pizza Hut pizza.

The importance of eating healthy foods is more important during a depressed state than at any other time. I suggest fresh fruit, lightly cooked vegetables, and a good serve of fish, chicken or lean steak. But giving nutritional advice is beyond the scope of this book and you will find plenty of nutrition information on the web.

In Potatoes Not Prozac, Kathleen Des Maisons PhD, an addiction and nutrition expert, recommends eating three main meals a day, and consuming mainly complex carbohydrates such as vegetables, whole grain foods and cereals. Grain should be sprouted grain.

She also advocates reducing or eliminating refined sugars (including alcohol) and restricting protein consumption to a serve no larger than your fist.

Furthermore she claims that many people, who are prone to addictive disorders as well as depression, are also sugar sensitive. Their body chemistry reacts in extreme ways to sugar and refined carbohydrates.

Sugar and refined carbohydrates change not only the blood sugar levels, but also the levels of serotonin and beta–endorphins in the brain, creating feelings of exhaustion, hopelessness and despair.

In his book The Great Australian Diet, Dr John Tickell discusses the eating habits of some of the most vital and longest living people in the world, the people of Okinawa, Japan.

Along with other Eastern cultures, the Okinawan diet is very high in vegetables/fruits/grains (85%) and fish (10%). Meat/poultry/dairy is a distant third (5%).

Although it is very hard to make direct comparisons because of cultural and healthcare delivery differences, the proportion of Okinawan people living with depression is much lower than that of Australians and other Western countries.

Meditation/Relaxation

To manage the frantic pace of modern life it is imperative to take time out and still the mind. This can sometimes seem very difficult when the mind is swamped with the negative thoughts that accompany depression. I personally practice Vedic Meditation.

Mastering the art of relaxation doesn't happen overnight, but like most things it improves with regular practice.

There are many relaxation MP3s and CDs available, quite often from local libraries. It is often best to try a few different ones and see which works best for you. Likewise, there are many different approaches to meditation.

Seek a teacher of Meditation or keep experimenting until you find a style that suits. I was fortunate to meet Thom Knoles who taught me a Vedic Meditation technique. I met Thom after I had survived most of my depressive episodes. Nevertheless I believe that learning meditation from Thom has helped me find bliss and stability and has helped me gain the inspiration and insight necessary, in the long run, to be able to write a book such as this one.

In his book, Full Catastrophe Living: How to cope with stress, pain and illness using mindfulness meditation, Jon Kabat Zinn, from the University of Massachusetts Medical Center, describes the excellent results he has achieved for stress and anxiety.

Mindfulness meditation is about living in the present moment and neither getting ahead of yourself, nor dwelling in the past. He guides participants through an eight week course of meditations.

Open ground (www.openground.com.au) is current;ly conducting online courses in Mindfulness Based Stress Reduction (MBSR.)

Professor Mark Williams, Zindel Segel and John Teasdale from the University of Wales have developed Mindfulness Based Cognitive Therapy (MBCT). They draw on Jon Kabat Zinn's Stress Reduction program.

The program includes simple breathing meditations and yoga stretches to help participants become more aware of the present moment, including getting in touch with moment-to-moment changes in the mind and the body.

MBCT includes basic education about depression and several exercises from cognitive therapy that show links between thinking and feeling and how participants can best look after themselves when depression threatens to overwhelm them.

MBCT has been used as a relapse prevention strategy with encouraging results. People who had suffered three or more episodes of depression before learning the practice reduced their relapse rate to 36% compared to 78% in the control group.

At the time of writing the first edition, The Black Dog Institute was involved in trials to evaluate how MBCT can help those in the midst of a depressive episode. Anecdotal feedback is encouraging. The Mindcare Centre (www.mindcare.com.au) also runs MBCT courses.

Now let's look at some other treatments available for depression:

Physical Treatments

The main physical treatments for depression comprise drug treatments and electroconvulsive therapy (ECT).

Because of its controversial past many people feel the need to think carefully before having ECT themselves or allowing it to be given to relatives. ECT has a small but important role in treatment, particularly in cases of: psychotic depression, severe melancholic depression where there is a high risk of suicide or the patient is too ill to eat, drink or take medications, life-threatening mania and severe post-natal depression

While there are some short-term side-effects, ECT is deemed relatively safe and, because an anaesthetic is used, deemed not too unpleasant.

A possible alternative to ECT is Transcranial Magnetic Stimulation (TMS). TMS has been a procedure used by neurologists, both as a treatment and a diagnostic strategy.

It consists of holding a coil next to the patient's head and creating a magnetic field to stimulate relevant parts of the brain. Unlike ECT, there is no need for a general anesthetic nor is a convulsion induced. The evidence in favor of this treatment is not yet in, but it is currently a major area of research.

A blog article by Dr Lindsay Israel on *successtms.com* reports various studies that demonstrate the many advantages that TMS has over ECT. These include:

- No hospitalization
- No anesthesia
- Non-invasive
- No major side effects
- Short recovery time

My suggested strategy for overcoming your depression:

1. Be awake and about during the day. Sunshine can work wonders.

2. Be sincerely grateful for everything you have, starting with having the eyes to read this.

3. Go for a walk, at least 10 minutes 3 times a week then increase the time and frequency.

4. Take the time to shop, prepare and eat healthy nourishing food.

5. Start to do the things that you've been neglecting, one at a time, one task each day e.g. tidy one room, do your laundry, washing up etc. Do just enough to give you a feeling of accomplishment.

6. Read some inspirational books, watch some inspirational movies.

7. Keep up your friendships and acquaintances and prevent social isolation.

8. Practice acts of kindness. Helping others is another way of helping yourself.

9. Practice regular meditation or prayer.

10. Consider taking the previously mentioned health supplements to accelerate your healing.

Conclusion

Congratulations on finishing this book. The exercises and techniques given to you will have helped you in some way or other. You may need to reread certain pages or do the exercises and techniques afresh. You may decide to seek professional help and that's fine too. I have done this myself in the past and it has been beneficial to me.

During my research while writing this book I looked at what others had to say on the subject of depression. In closing this book I will therefore include an excerpt from an article I found online. The article is by Maria Sobrado, a Life Coach:

"Long term depression has to be experienced to be believed and if you suffer from it, you know what I'm talking about. You look around you and see yourself living in a world where you feel you don't belong. You wonder how everyone else gets up and faces the day filled with vim and vigor and the tenacity to get going. While you have to work extra hard to get out of bed and take a shower! Little tasks seem daunting. You lose concentration. Nothing you do ever feels right.

There is an underlying feeling that never goes away no matter how many sticks you shake at it. No matter how many books you read about it. No matter how many doctors you talk to about it. Even the pills you've tried over the years do nothing. You begin to feel that this is just how your life will be. You've stopped talking to friends about your feelings and have decided to accept it and work with it, end of sentence, done.

You may have noticed that your depression comes in waves and there are times when you catch yourself feeling happy or different and you wonder how you can keep up the good work. How can I be like everyone else? What happened in that moment, where for a second or a minute or an hour I lost myself in time and felt peaceful?

How did you do it? I want you to remember the last time you felt happy, even if it was a few years ago, or a minute ago! What initiated the moment? Seriously, think about it, write it down, feel it again, then smile about it! I know you can catch yourself smiling in odd moments even in your depression. I've spoken to people and heard the smile in their voice while they were in the midst of the worst moments of deep depression. We all have a smile hiding somewhere inside that we can pull out at a moment's notice, especially when we are not focused on ourselves.

That's right, I said it! When we aren't focused on ourselves we can light up a room! When we can pull ourselves forward and focus on something outside we can flip the switch in an instant! I bring this up for a reason and it's not to tell you to go out and start volunteering to help others, although that is an unconventional way to deal with long term depression. I mention it to call notice to what is inside of you. I believe that every single person has control over their own emotional well being in every moment of every day and to state otherwise about yourself is the difference between experiencing normal moments of depression aka sadness (that everyone has) and letting it continue on and on for months and years of your life.

I have read or been told that depression is unexpressed anger turned inward. This makes sense to me up to a point. As a long term "depressionista" I have noticed that I can get pretty angry when no one understands what I'm feeling and I can get pretty angry that my life feels the same way, where the anger turned inward comes in is the stuck part where I feel as if there is nothing I can do to change it. But, I can. But I don't want to because I'm depressed! But, I can, but I don't want to because I'm tired! But, I can and the "buts" stops there, honestly, it does!

So what can you do?

- Go ahead, have a good long cry. Some of the healthiest people I know cry at the drop of a hat. They happy cry. They sad cry! The point is they cry! When they feel it, they let it out. Depression is really unexpressed emotion.

- Go ahead get angry! Have at it. Call up a friend or a coach or the dog and ask permission to go on a raging rant! See if you can make it last more than 10 minutes. Seriously get out a timer, then, get it off your chest. If you can't find anyone, get out your journal and get writing. Can you write your anger down for 10 minutes?

- Get physical! Yeah, I know! Who has the energy to punch a pillow? Try it, you might like it! Physical movement is the best way to move depressed energy. If you don't believe me, ask a jogger.

- If you really can't get out of bed or off the couch try crossing the room to insert the funniest movie you can find into your DVD and press play. Watch, laugh, rinse and repeat.

I'm not sure if you've noticed, but these unconventional methods should be used to get you out of your state of depression in the moment.

So you realize that depression is a state of mind that can be conquered when you put forth some effort. And, it's an effort you've used before but haven't paid attention to.

You will probably want to get to the root of these problems with the assistance of a qualified professional, but in the meantime actually use some of these methods and you will begin to understand that it's always about what you decide to do that will make the difference between long term depression and the moments of sadness we all experience."

Other Books By this Author

➢ Anxiety Self Help: How to overcome anxiety
➢ The Secrets to Healthy Self Esteem: How to repair and Improve Your Self Esteem

Recommended Reading

Doidge, Norman - *The Brain That Changes Itself,* Scribe Publications, 1 March 2010

McKay, Matthew and Patrick Fanning - *Self-Esteem,* New Harbinger Publications Inc.

Wehrenberg, Margaret - *The 10 Best-Ever Depression Management Techniques,* W.W.Norton & Company. New York, London

Seligman, Martin Dr. - *Learned Optimism: How to change your mind and your life,* Paperback reprint edition, Penguin Books, 1998

Yapko, Michael - *Breaking the Patterns of Depression,* Broadway Books New York

References

Diagnostic and Statistical Manual of Mental Disorders

Major Depressive Disorder - *en.wikipedia.com*

Beyond Blue - *www.beyondblue.com.au*

Dr Mercola Newsletter - *www.mercola.com*

Rossi, Ernest Dr - *Australian Journal of Clinical Hypnotherapy and Hypnosis,* Sept 2009

Seligman, Martin Dr - *University of Pennsylvania Positive Psychology Center*

Study from - *Duke University*, North Carolina 2001

Israel, Lindsay, Dr - *American Journal of Preventative Medicine,* Jan 2005

Cooper Centre Longitudinal Study - *Cooper Research Research Institute* Dallas Texas

Dunn, Andrea - *American Journal of Preventative Medicine,* Jan 2005

Des Maisons, Kathleen, Phd - *Potatoes and Prozac: Solutions for sugar sensitivity,* Jan 2008

Tickell, John Dr - *Food and Nutrition in Australia* - Edited by Mark L Walhlqvist, Third Edition, Thomas Nelson Australia 1988

Jon Kabat Zinn - *Full Catastrophe of Living: How to cope with pain, stress and illness using mindfulness meditation,* Feb 1, 2001

Williams, Mark et al - *Mindfulness Based Cognitive Therapy for Depression*

Black Dog Institute - *www.blackdoginstitute.org.au*

Israel, Lindsay Dr. - *www.successtms.com*, Jan 15, 2020

Knoles, Thom - *www.thomknoles.com*

Bach, Donna N.D. et Al - *Journal of Integrative Medicine*, Feb 19. 2019

www.ingramcontent.com/pod-product-compliance
Lightning Source LLC
Chambersburg PA
CBHW070614060426

42445CB00038B/1173